EXPLORE
FORCES
AND
MOTION!

Jennifer Swanson

Illustrated by Bryan Stone

Recent science titles in the **Explore Your World!** Series

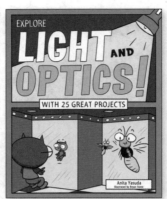
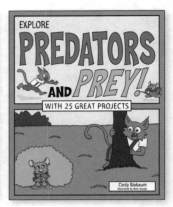

Check out more titles at www.nomadpress.net

Nomad Press
A division of Nomad Communications
10 9 8 7 6 5 4 3 2 1

This book was manufactured by Marquis Book Printing,
Montmagny, Québec, Canada
June 2016, Job #121613

ISBN Softcover: 978-1-61930-355-3
ISBN Hardcover: 978-1-61930-351-5

Educational Consultant, Marla Conn

Questions regarding the ordering of this book should be addressed to
Nomad Press
2456 Christian St.
White River Junction, VT 05001
www.nomadpress.net

Printed in Canada.

CONTENTS

PS **Interested in primary sources? Look for this icon.**
Use a smartphone or tablet app to scan the QR code and explore more!
You can find a list of URLs on the Resources page.

If the QR code doesn't work, try searching the Internet
with the Keyword Prompts to find other helpful sources.

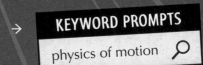

KEYWORD PROMPTS

physics of motion 🔍

300s BCE: Aristotle, an ancient Greek, develops the first theory of physics. He also comes up with ideas about gravity and motion.

200s BCE: Archimedes, also an ancient Greek, develops his principle for buoyancy. He also is the first to explain levers as simple machines.

1630: Johannes Kepler develops a theory on how the planets move in space.

1600: Galileo discovers inertia, which eventually becomes Newton's first law of motion.

1543: Copernicus publishes a paper on how forces work to pull planets together. He says that the sun is the center of the universe.

1686: Isaac Newton presents his three laws of motion that govern everything that happens on earth.

1800: Alessandro Volta invents the electric battery.

1831: Michael Faraday discovers electromagnetic induction, the principles of the first motor and generator.

TIMELINE

10 BCE: Heron, another ancient Greek, uses mathematics to prove ideas in physics and creates many machines, including a programmable robot.

1000 CE: Shen Kuo, a Chinese physicist, works with a compass and discovers that it points to the magnetic north of the earth, not true north.

1200: French scientist Petrus Peregrinus writes about the forces acting on a magnet and how they interact with the earth, which is one giant magnet.

1040: The teachings of ancient Greece were nearly lost during centuries of war, but the Arabs have preserved them. Ibn al-Haytham, called Alhazen, is an Arab doctor who is the first to study light and how it works.

1859: James Clerk Maxwell comes up with a theory about the electromagnetic field.

1905: Albert Einstein develops his special theory of relativity to explain the forces and motion that act within the universe.

1903: Marie and Pierre Curie are awarded a Nobel Prize for their research in radioactivity.

2012: The Higgs boson particle is discovered in the Large Hadron Collider. This is a step toward understanding what makes up the entire universe.

INTRODUCTION

EVERYTHING MOVES!

You have had a long day. School was busy. You had a test in one class and a quiz in another, and you had soccer practice in the afternoon. Time to rest! You flop down in your comfy chair with a book, ready to just not move for a while. Have you ever felt like that? Did you know that while you were sitting in that big comfy chair, you were actually still moving?

In this book, we will discuss how everything moves all the time! You, your bike, the earth, and a hockey puck that glides across the ice are all in motion. What changes this movement? A force.

WORDS TO KNOW

motion: the action or process of moving or changing place or position.

force: a push or pull applied to an object.

Have you ever kicked a soccer ball? Pushed someone on a swing? Picked up a box and carried it to a table? Then you have experienced forces and motion.

gravity: a force that pushes down on objects and also pulls things together in space.

pressure: a force acting on a surface from an object or fluid. Air is considered a fluid.

WORDS TO KNOW

What is a force? A force is simply a push or a pull. You can't see a force, but you can see the effect that a force has on an object.

Forces change the way things move. This movement is called motion. Forces and motion go together. If you push something, it moves away from you. If you pull it, the object moves toward you. When you push someone on the swing, your hands are acting as the force.

Forces still act on you when you are sitting still. Gravity and pressure from the air are pushing on you while your body is pushing back! These forces are balanced. When forces are balanced, it can seem like there is no motion.

Motion happens when forces are unbalanced. When you kick a soccer ball, the force comes from your foot hitting the ball. That force makes the ball move across the field.

Forces can make objects speed up, slow down, or change direction. They can even make an object sink or float. Forces and motion rule the world.

ISAAC NEWTON

Isaac Newton (1643–1727) is one of the most famous and important scientists of all time. Some say he discovered gravity when an apple fell on his head. While that is probably more fiction than fact, Newton was the first scientist to explain how gravity works. Newton was an excellent mathematician, too. He used his expertise in math and science to develop the three laws of motion that rule the universe. Newton's work with forces and motion paved the way for scientists to discover how they affect every part of human life!

There are many different forces that affect motion. Have you ever wondered why you always fall down and never fall up? Gravity is the force that pulls you to the ground! Magnetism is a force that attracts, but also repels. Have you ever wondered how things float? It's a force called buoyancy. And why do we make footprints when we walk in sand or snow? Your feet are applying pressure to the ground.

The push and pull of every object on the planet and in space is caused by the way a force acts upon it. Forces are so important to everyday life that a scientist named Sir Isaac Newton, who lived in the seventeenth century, created three laws to describe exactly how forces and motion work.

WORDS TO KNOW

magnetism: the force that attracts or repels between magnets.

attract: a force that draws things closer, usually applied to a magnet.

repel: a force that pushes things away, usually applied to a magnet.

buoyancy: the force that makes something able to float in a liquid or gas.

3

orbit: the path of an object circling another object in space.

property: a quality or feature of something. The way something is.

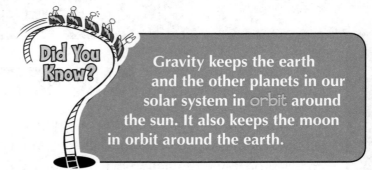

Gravity keeps the earth and the other planets in our solar system in orbit around the sun. It also keeps the moon in orbit around the earth.

In this book, you will explore how forces and motion work on us and through us every day. You'll learn more about Newton's three laws of motion. And you'll become a junior physicist as you perform hands-on experiments that show the ups and downs, pushes and pulls, and even the gravity-defying properties of forces and motion. So get ready to get moving and see forces and motion in action!

PUSH ME PULL YOU

Since we can't see forces, the best way to learn about forces is to feel them. Try this quick activity to feel a force.

* Ask a partner to help you.

* Draw a line or lay a stick across the sidewalk or in the grass.

* You stand on one side. Your partner stands on the other.

* Grab hands across the line.

* Try to pull your partner across the line. The person being pulled should resist.

What does this feel like? What is happening between the two of you?

GOOD SCIENCE PRACTICES

Each chapter of this book begins with a question to help guide your exploration of forces and motion. Keep the question in your mind as you read the chapter. At the end of each chapter, use your science journal to record your thoughts and answer.

INVESTIGATE!

What is the relationship between force and motion?

Step	Example
1. Question: What are we trying to find out? What problem are we trying to solve?	Is gravity a strong enough force to bring me back to the ground after I jump off a stool?
2. Research: What do other people think?	Books at the library explain that gravity is the force that keeps me on Earth.
3. Hypothesis/Prediction: What do we think the answer will be?	I think that gravity will bring me back to the ground after I jump off the stool.
4. Equipment: What supplies are we using?	A small stool, sneakers, science journal, and pencil
5. Method: What procedure are we following?	Jump from the stool five times.
6. Results: What happened and why?	Do you land on the ground every time? If so, gravity is a strong enough force to return you to the ground! Record your results.

Every good scientist keeps a science journal! Choose a notebook to use as your science journal. As you read through this book and do the activities, keep track of your observations in a scientific method worksheet, like the one shown here. Scientists use the scientific method to keep their experiments organized.

SUPPLIES

* 4 books
* package of index cards
* handful of coins
* scissors
* science journal and pencil

BUILDING BRIDGES

Forces act on everything, even things that are standing still. Engineers need to understand forces when they build structures such as bridges. Let's see how different bridges support the forces that are placed upon them.

1 Make two stacks of two books each. The stacks should be the same height and close together.

2 Balance an index card between the stacks, with about ½ inch of the card on each stack to form a small bridge.

3 How many coins will this bridge support? Start a scientific method worksheet in your science journal. What is your hypothesis?

4 Stack up coins until your bridge collapses. Record the number of coins in your notebook.

WORDS TO KNOW

engineer: someone who uses science, math, and creativity to design products or processes to meet human needs or solve problems.

5 Repeat the experiment, but this time try to make your bridge stronger. You can pile more cards on top, bend the cards in any shape, or cut them to fill in the bridge, but you cannot use any other materials. What else can you do to improve your bridge?

physics: the science of how matter and energy work together.

matter: what an object is made of.

energy: the ability to do **work**.

work: the amount of energy needed to move an object a certain distance.

═ WORDS TO KNOW ═

6 Record your results for each type of bridge you create.

THINK ABOUT IT: The force of the cards pushing up must be equal to or greater than the force of the coins pushing down. What's the best way to increase the amount of force pushing up?

WHAT IS PHYSICS?

Physics is from the ancient Greek word *phusis*. The word *physics* means "nature," but not nature as in plants and animals. *Physics* means "nature" as in the nature of how things work. It is the study of **matter**, the tiny bits that make up everything in the universe. Physics is the study of how matter and **energy** are affected by forces and motion in space and on the earth.

With an adult's permission, watch the videos on this YouTube channel to learn lots more about physics!

KEYWORD PROMPTS

minute physics video 🔍

CHAPTER ONE

FANTASTIC FORCES

Forces are all around you. They act on everything and everyone every single day of our lives. For the most part, you probably don't even notice forces, because they are invisible. But every time you push open a door, you are experiencing a force. Every time you walk across the room or kick a ball in the goal, you are experiencing a force.

? INVESTIGATE!

What would it be like to live in a world that had no forces at all?

normal force: the support force pushing outward from an object.

WORDS TO KNOW

BALANCING ACT

As you sit and read this book, at least four different forces are acting upon you. Gravity is pulling you down, while the ground is pushing you up. The air all around you is squeezing in on you, but the matter inside your body is pushing back.

Did You Know?

Forces are measured in units called Newtons and are named for the famous scientist Isaac Newton, not the Fig Newton cookie!

You don't feel all of these forces because they are balanced. That means the gravity force pulling you down is equal to the force from the ground that is pushing you up, called the **normal force**. When you push on a wall, it doesn't collapse because the normal force pushes back.

If one of the forces was stronger than the others, you would probably feel it. For example, if the gravity force was stronger than the normal force, your feet might sink into the soil. That would make it pretty hard to walk!

But if the normal force were greater than gravity, you might float a few inches off the ground.

STRONGER NORMAL FORCE

STRONGER GRAVITY FORCE

9

ALBERT EINSTEIN

Albert Einstein (1879–1955) is one of the most famous physicists who has ever lived. A physicist is a scientist who studies the world around us to learn about its basic laws, such as gravity. These basic laws tell us how things work and interact. Physicists study the earth, space, the planets and stars, above and beneath the water, and different materials and how they behave. Physicists can be teachers or engineers. They can work with computers or even work in business and finance. Albert Einstein created **theories** that explain how things work on the earth and in space.

Forces work in pairs. When you pull a rubber band, it stretches. But the rubber in the band also pulls back against you. The two forces are a pair. What happens if you let go? The rubber band will bounce back to its original shape. If you pull the rubber band too hard, then it will snap.

Forces also make things move. Forces are what make everything go. Cars, bicycles, basketballs, and airplanes all make us think of motion. Motion is also a part of our own activities, such as walking, running, and jumping.

Motion happens when an object changes position or location. The best example is you. Every time you move your legs to walk, you are using force to put yourself into motion. Imagine you are pushing your friend on the swing. When you push her gently, she only moves a little. But when you give her a big push, she swings way up high. The amount of force that you apply to an object is directly related to how much you can change the motion.

WORDS TO KNOW

theory: a set of ideas to explain something that has happened.

NEAR AND FAR FORCES

Some forces act from a distance, which means they do not have to be in direct contact with the object. Gravity and magnetism are two examples of this kind of force. Gravity acts upon everything all the time. If you are on the earth, you can't get away from gravity.

Magnetism is a force that acts between two magnets. It can either attract and pull the magnets together, or it can repel and push the magnets apart. Magnets do not need to be touching for this force to happen. They have an invisible field around them called the **magnetic field**. This is what allows the attracting and repelling to happen.

magnetic field: the space near a magnet where the magnetic force is felt.

lodestone: a naturally magnetized piece of rock.

contact force: a force that occurs when two objects are touching each other.

applied force: a force that is applied to an object by a person or another object.

WORDS TO KNOW

Did You Know?

The word *magnet* is from the ancient Greek word "Magnes." This was the name of the region where magnetized ore called lodestone was mined.

Some forces require the objects to be touching in order for them to act upon the object. These are called **contact forces**. They include the following forces.

NORMAL FORCE: The normal force is the one that pushes up from the ground. It opposes gravity and keeps us from sinking into the soil.

APPLIED FORCE: An **applied force** is one that is applied to an object. The best example is you holding this book. You are applying a force with your hands to the book, which keeps the book from falling to the ground because of gravity.

friction: a force that slows down objects when they rub against each other. Friction acts in opposition to movement.

tension force: a force transmitted through a string or rope.

spring force: a force exerted by a compressed or stretched spring.

compress: pressed or pushed into less space than normal.

resisting force: a force that pushes back on an object, usually by air or water.

air resistance: the force of air pushing against an object.

WORDS TO KNOW

FRICTIONAL FORCE: Friction is the force that happens when two objects are rubbed against each other. Take both of your hands and hold them together. Now rub them back and forth. Do you feel resistance between your palms? That is friction. Friction is what makes things slow down.

TENSION FORCE: Tension force is a pulling force that is caused by a string or cable or chain on another object. Think of a dog wearing a leash. As the dog pulls on the leash, he is creating tension. You feel that tensional force in your hand and it makes you pull back on the leash.

SPRING FORCE: A spring force is created by a compressed spring. Have you ever jumped on a trampoline? As you jump, the trampoline bends downward, but then it bounces right back up. The trampoline bending and rebounding is a spring force.

RESISTING FORCE: A resisting force is caused by air pushing on an object. Imagine you are walking into the wind on a windy day. Can you feel the wind pushing against you? The air resistance makes it harder to walk forward. If the wind is at your back, the resistance pushes you along and makes walking easier.

RESISTANCE IS FUTILE!

Air resistance depends on the size and shape of an object. The greater the **surface area** of an object, the more air resistance it experiences. That is why planes and rockets are shaped like long cones—to reduce air resistance. Can you imagine an airplane shaped like a box trying to fly? What might happen to it?

WORDS TO KNOW

surface area: the total area on the surface of an object.

Many forces can act on an object at the same time. If you were to push a box across the floor, there are at least four forces that are occurring simultaneously. Can you name them? Only when one force is unbalanced can the object be moved.

If two forces acting in the opposite direction are equal, they will cancel each other out. If you push on a box, and someone else pushes on the box with the same amount of force, the box will not move.

What about a tug of war? If both sides pull with an equal amount of force, no one will win. Only when one side pulls with a greater force will the rope move.

Forces control most of what we do, but the force we deal with all the time on earth and in space is gravity. We'll find out how much effect glorious gravity has on you in the next chapter!

? INVESTIGATE!

It's time to consider and discuss: What would it be like to live in a world that had no forces at all?

SLOW IT DOWN!

Friction is a force between two objects that slows things down. Let's see how weight, the type of surface, and the strength of the movement affect friction.

SUPPLIES

✳ science journal and pencil
✳ empty box
✳ 3 books
✳ smooth wood or tile floor or smooth tabletop
✳ blanket

1 Start a scientific method worksheet in your science journal. What is your hypothesis? How hard will it be to move the box across the floor or table? How hard will it be to move it across the blanket? Organize your experiment in a chart like this.

Method	Prediction	Result
Empty box, smooth surface		
Books in box, smooth surface		
Empty box, blanket surface		
Books in box, blanket surface		

2 Place the empty box on the smooth table or floor. Push the empty box across the floor with both of your hands. How easy is that to do? Record your observations in your science journal.

3 Now put the books inside the box. Push the box across the floor or table again. Was it harder?

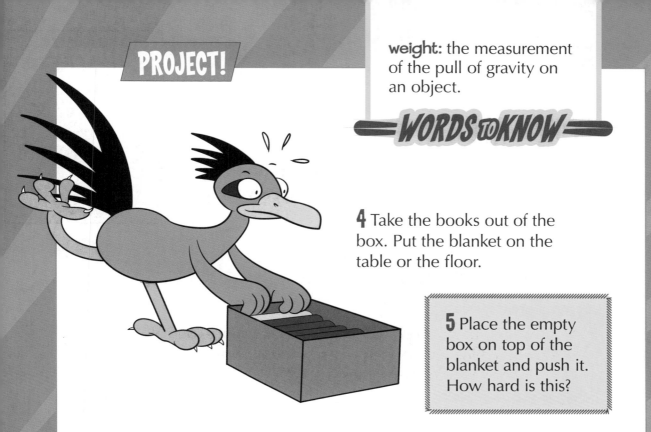

weight: the measurement of the pull of gravity on an object.

WORDS TO KNOW

4 Take the books out of the box. Put the blanket on the table or the floor.

5 Place the empty box on top of the blanket and push it. How hard is this?

6 Put the books back into the box and push the box across the blanket. Is this harder or easier that all the other ways you tried?

WHAT IS HAPPENING? Friction is affected by the **weight** of the object and also by the surface that the object is resting upon. When the box was empty, pushing it across the smooth surface was pretty easy. When you added the books, you increased the weight. This meant you had to push harder and apply more force to move it. The same thing goes for pushing the box across the blanket. The empty box required more force to push it across the blanket. The blanket, unlike the floor or table, has a rough surface, which creates more friction and slows the box down.

What forces are acting on the box when you push it? What force has to increase to get the box to move? What force has to be overcome?

SUPPLIES

* paper clip
* piece of thread
* tape
* science journal and pencil
* magnet

FLYING PAPER CLIP

A magnetic force is invisible, but it can be very strong. Let's see how it can make this paper clip appear to fly.

1 Tie the piece of thread to the paper clip. Tape the other end of the thread to the table.

2 Start a scientific method worksheet in your science journal. What do you think will happen when you hold a magnet near the paper clip? What is your hypothesis?

3 Hold the magnet just above the paper clip. What happens to the paper clip?

4 Try holding the magnet on all different sides of the paper clip without touching it. What does the paper clip do? Record your observations in your journal.

WHAT IS HAPPENING? The metal in the paper clip is attracted to the magnet. The magnet has an invisible field around it called the magnetic field that attracts the paper clip without actually having to touch it. Try your magnet on other materials, such as other kinds of metal, plastic, paper, and dirt. What happens?

HOW DID THE ROCKET LOSE ITS JOB?

HA HA HA HA

It was fired.

CRUMPLED OR SQUARE?

The surface area of an object can affect the amount of friction it experiences. Let's see how it affects this piece of paper.

1 Crumple one sheet of paper. Fold another sheet of paper. Leave the last sheet of paper flat.

2 Drop them at the same time from the same height. Which one lands first? Why?

WHAT IS HAPPENING? You will see that the crumpled paper lands first. The reason is because it has less surface area, which means it experiences less air resistance. The flat sheet of paper has more air resistance, which prevents it from falling as fast. What happened to the folded piece of paper? Why?

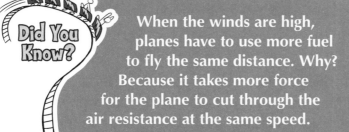

Did You Know?

When the winds are high, planes have to use more fuel to fly the same distance. Why? Because it takes more force for the plane to cut through the air resistance at the same speed.

BOOK BUDDIES

Friction can be a weak force, such as a wheel sliding across the ice. It can be a strong force when many forces are added together. Let's see how this works.

1 Open the notebooks on the flat surface. Take one page from one of the notebooks and lay it on the other.

2 Alternate placing the pages between the other pages of the notebook until the notebooks are completely intertwined.

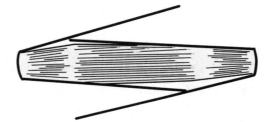

3 Create a scientific method worksheet in your science journal. What do you think will happen when you try to pull the notebooks apart?

4 With a friend, each of you pick up a notebook. Try to pull them apart. Can you?

WHAT IS HAPPENING? The intertwined pages create lots of friction against each other. This friction is so strong that it prevents you from pulling the two books apart. The reason why the friction is so strong is because it is added together. Two pages intertwined don't have a lot of friction, but hundreds of pages intertwined lead to a huge amount of friction!

CHAPTER TWO

GLORIOUS GRAVITY

Gravity is the force that keeps you on the ground. Without it, you'd fly right off the earth! Gravity affects everything. It affects cars, balls, feathers, ships, buildings, planets, and even you. Gravity is the one force you can never get away from. Everywhere you go, you are affected by gravity.

Have you ever been running along on the sidewalk and tripped? What happens? You fall! That's gravity acting upon you. Gravity is the force that pulls an object toward the center of the earth.

 INVESTIGATE!

Could you live on the earth without gravity?

mass: how much matter is in an object.

gravitational force: the force of gravity, measured in Newtons.

WORDS TO KNOW

There is a legend that says Sir Isaac Newton discovered gravity when an apple fell from a tree and hit him on the head. Isaac thought that the force that caused the apple to drop is the same force that holds the universe together. He was right, and we call this force gravity.

Gravity is an invisible force of attraction between two objects. The objects can be you and the earth, a ball and the ground, or two planets. Gravity acts on objects that have mass. Mass is the amount of matter that makes up an object.

Even though we can't see gravity, we can feel it. You may not have felt the pull of gravity as you fell to the ground after tripping, but if you jumped out of a plane and dropped to the ground with a parachute, you'd feel it. The pull of gravity is called the gravitational force.

Gravitational force is measured in terms of weight. Weight and mass are not the same things. Your mass is how much matter makes up your body. Regardless of where you are—on the ground, in space, or deep in the ocean—your mass stays the same.

Your weight, however, depends on the amount of gravitational force that is being exerted upon your body. Your weight is measured by how hard gravity is pulling on you.

GALILEO'S EXPERIMENT

WHAT GOES UP BUT DOES NOT MOVE?

HA HA HA HA

Stairs.

How do you know how hard gravity is pulling on you? The famous physicist, engineer, and scientist Galileo Galilei wondered that same thing. Galileo lived in Pisa, Italy, in the late 1500s.

Back then, not many people understood the force of gravity. Galileo knew that gravity was the force that made objects fall to the ground, but he still had questions. Did the mass of an object affect the speed of its fall? Would a heavy object fall faster than a light object when they were both dropped from the same height? He decided to find out.

Galileo climbed 294 steps to the top of the famous leaning Tower of Pisa to test his theory. In his hands, he held two balls. Both balls were similar in size but different in mass—one was heavier than the other. He dropped the balls at the same moment. Galileo expected the heavier ball to fall faster. What do you think happened?

As Galileo watched, the two balls fell at the same speed and landed on the ground at the same time. But how was that possible? Shouldn't the heavier ball fall faster? As Galileo learned, the gravitational force on all objects on the earth is the same, regardless of their mass.

He repeated the experiment again and again, measuring the rate of descent of the balls. He calculated that each ball fell from the top of the tower at the same speed.

While all objects do fall at the same rate, sometimes other forces interfere with the descent. For example, if Galileo were to try his experiment again with an apple and a feather, do you think they would hit the ground at the same time? What do you think would happen instead?

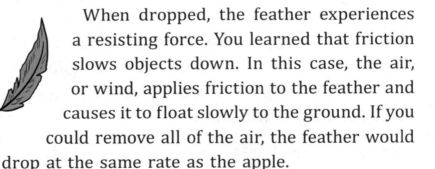

When dropped, the feather experiences a resisting force. You learned that friction slows objects down. In this case, the air, or wind, applies friction to the feather and causes it to float slowly to the ground. If you could remove all of the air, the feather would drop at the same rate as the apple.

BOWLING BALL VS. FEATHER

It takes a special room and special equipment to create an airless chamber, but that's what you need to see the true nature of gravity. **You can watch it here.**

KEYWORD PROMPTS

feather bowling ball same speed 🔍 ←

GALILEO GALILEI

Galileo Galilei (1564–1642) was an Italian mathematician, scientist, and astronomer who is often called the "father of modern science." Galileo was the first to develop a working telescope, which he used to study the stars and the planets. With his telescope, Galileo proved that the sun was the center of the solar system. He said that the planets revolved around the sun instead of the sun moving around the earth. This was a new idea and went against everything that people knew at the time. Still, Galileo believed it to be true and wrote his own book about it. He turned out to be right.

Galileo's research of air resistance and its affect upon gravity are important. This explains how parachutes work. If you drop a rock out of an airplane, it's going to fall very fast toward the ground. The same thing happens to a person! When a person first jumps out of the plane, they begin accelerating downward. Then they pull a cord and their parachute releases. The parachute slows them down so they can descend at a slower, more controlled rate.

accelerate: to change the speed of an object over time.

Gravity is not just the force of attraction between objects and the earth. It is also the attraction between two objects. Sir Isaac Newton, the famous physicist from the 1600s, determined that every object in the universe has some type of gravitational force upon every other object. He wrote three laws to describe gravity and motion, which you'll learn about in the next chapter.

Did You Know?

The sun accounts for 99.86 percent of the weight of our entire solar system.

Why don't you feel the gravitational force between you and your desk? Only forces produced by big things, such as the sun, the earth, the moon, or another planet, can be felt. This is because the more mass an object has, the greater the force of attraction.

GRAVITY IN SPACE

The pull of the earth's gravity keeps the moon in orbit around the earth. The moon can feel the earth's pull because the earth and the moon are such huge objects.

The sun is the largest and most massive object in our solar system. It's 864,938 miles across! That is the same distance as 109 earths lined up next to each other. The amount of gravitational force the sun exerts is huge. It is the one force that keeps all eight planets in their individual orbits.

What about when we see videos of astronauts in space? Don't they look like they're floating without any gravity?

HOW MUCH DO YOU WEIGH?

Each planet has its own gravitational force. Some planets have a greater force of gravity than Earth and some have less. The force of gravity is measured by an object's weight.

Multiply your weight by the number for each planet below. This would be your weight on that planet. On which planet will you be able to jump the highest?

* Mercury: 0.38   * Earth: 1.00   * Jupiter: 2.34   * Uranus: 0.92

* Venus: 0.91   * Mars: 0.38   * Saturn: 1.06   * Neptune: 1.19

free fall: the motion of an object being acted upon only by the force of gravity, such as if it were falling from the sky.

atmosphere: the blanket of air surrounding the earth.

WORDS TO KNOW

Remember, the greater the mass, the greater the gravitational pull. Astronauts are very small compared to the sun and the earth. Also, gravity decreases with distance. Astronauts are hundreds of millions of miles away from the sun. Therefore, astronauts don't feel a noticeable pull from the sun.

Even though they might not feel it, astronauts, just like their spaceships, are in continuous **free fall**. This means they are falling toward the earth. The reason they don't hit the ground is that they are above the earth's **atmosphere**.

If an astronaut fell far enough to reach the outer edges of the earth's atmosphere, they would fall like a skydiver does. With an adult's permission, find an online video of the space shuttle coming back to earth. It needed a giant parachute to slow it down.

INVESTIGATE!

It's time to consider and discuss: Could you live on the earth without gravity?

* 2 balls of the same size but different mass (one weighs more than the other)
* stepladder or stool
* partner
* tape measure
* science journal and pencil

TRY GALILEO'S EXPERIMENT

Does a heavy object fall faster than a lighter one? This was Galileo's question when he climbed to the top of the Tower of Pisa. Try to do Galileo's experiment and see if you come to the same conclusions as he did.

Caution: Make sure you have an adult's permission to use the stepladder or stool. Have another person stand next to you to keep you from falling.

1 Climb the ladder or step stool with the two balls.

2 Hold the balls at arm's length away from your body at the same height. Have your partner measure the height of the balls from the ground. Record the height in your science journal.

3 Drop both balls at the same time. Watch them fall. Did they both hit the ground at the same time? If not, which one hit first? Repeat steps 1 to 3 a few times and write down the results in your journal. Did you get the same results as Galileo?

THINK ABOUT IT: Repeat the experiment using a video camera to record the dropped balls. Do you see anything different when you play it back in slow motion? Did you drop the two balls at exactly the same moment every time? Did the balls both hit the ground at the same time? Were you able to repeat your results? If the two balls you chose were close in size, do you think something heavier would fall faster?

WEIGHTLESS WATER

What happens when you drop two objects from the same height, but one of those objects is inside the other? This project is best done outside!

1 Poke a hole in the cup on the side near the bottom. Put your finger over the hole and pour water into the cup. What do you think will happen when you remove your finger?

2 Take your finger off. What happens to the water? Does it flow out in a steady stream? Write down your observations in your science journal.

3 What will happen if you do the experiment again but drop the cup at the same time you take your finger off the hole? Write down your hypothesis in your science journal.

4 Hold your finger over the hole in the cup again and fill it back up with water. This time, drop the cup at the same time as you let go of the hole. What happens to the water? Why?

WHAT IS HAPPENING? Think about gravity. When you first held the cup and took your finger off the hole, the water came straight out due to gravity. But when you dropped the cup, the water and the cup are dropping at the same speed and, for a second, both are considered to be weightless. That means that the water should stay inside the cup, until it hits the ground. Then, splash! Can you capture it on video?

MAKE YOUR OWN PARACHUTE

Parachutes work because they use air resistance to control the fall. In this activity, you'll design and construct your own parachute. The goal is to make it fall slowly so that the weight, which represents a person, lands gently on the ground.

SUPPLIES

* ✳ plastic bag or light material that is a bit flimsy, not hard
* ✳ scissors
* ✳ string
* ✳ a small object to act as the weight, such as a small action figure
* ✳ science journal and pencil
* ✳ timer (optional)

1 Cut out a large square from your plastic bag or material. Trim the edges so it looks like an octagon, which is an eight-sided shape.

2 Cut a small hole about ½ inch in from each edge. Attach eight pieces of string of the same length to each of the holes.

3 Tie the strings together and attach the end of them to your weight.

4 Use a chair or find a high spot to drop your parachute. Where can you get high enough so the parachute encounters lots of air resistance?

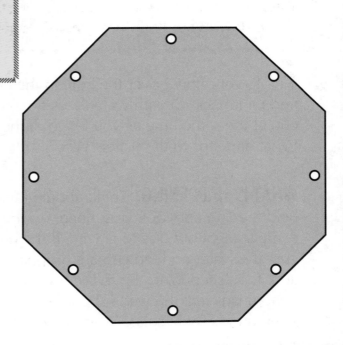

5 Let your parachute go! Observe its descent and record your observations in your science journal. Repeat this experiment six to eight times. You can use a timer to measure how long the parachute stays in the air.

WHAT IS HAPPENING? Did your parachute fall slowly? Or did it drop to the ground quickly? How hard did the weight hit the ground? Remember that the weight represents a person. What could you do to make the landing softer? Did the parachute fall in a straight line or did it fly sideways? What can you do to the parachute to make it fall straight down? **Watch an animated example of how a parachute works here.**

KEYWORD PROMPTS

how does a parachute work video 🔍

SUPER-HIGH SKYDIVE

The highest skydive was made in 2014 by Alan Eustace. He rode a high-altitude balloon to 135,890 feet, just more than 25 miles, above the surface of the earth. Then he let go of the balloon so he could fall back to the ground.

You can watch him perform this amazing feat here.

KEYWORD PROMPTS

Alan Eustace video 🔍

SUPPLIES

* plastic bucket
* water
* outdoor space
* science journal and pencil

CAN GRAVITY BE IGNORED?

Gravity is the most important force on the earth. The force of gravity from the moon and the sun even cause the tides in the ocean! But there is one other type of force that can overcome it—at least for a few seconds.

Caution: This activity is best done outside in a large area.

1 Fill the bucket about a quarter full of water. Turn the bucket upside down. What happens? The water falls out due to gravity, right?

2 Now, refill the bucket one quarter full. What do you think will happen if you turn the bucket upside down again, but this time you swing the bucket in a circle over your head? Record your predictions in your science journal.

WHY DID THE BIRD GET A TICKET?

HA HA HA HA

Because he broke the law of gravity!

perpendicular: when an object forms a right angle with another object.

centripetal force: the tendency of an object following a curved path to move away from the center of the curve.

WORDS TO KNOW

3 Keeping your arm straight, lift the bucket and begin twirling it around with your arm. Move your arm in a circle **perpendicular** to the ground. What happens to the water?

WHAT IS HAPPENING? Centripetal force is keeping the water inside the bucket. Centripetal force is the tendency of an object following a curved path to move away from the center of the curve. In this case, your arm is the curved path and your shoulder is the center of the curve. Your shoulder is the point from which the water will move away.

CURVED PATH OF BUCKET

CENTER OF THE CURVE

CENTRIPETAL FORCE PUSHING WATER OUTWARD

CHAPTER THREE

LAWS OF MOTION

History is full of scientists and scholars who have studied forces and motion. Aristotle suggested that stones fall to the earth because they are made of the same substance. The Greek astronomer Ptolemy argued that the earth is made of the heaviest of four natural elements of earth, water, air, and fire. Because of this, he believed that the earth sits in the center of the universe, with all the planets and stars moving around it in perfect circles. While these theories turned out to be wrong, for many years people believed them!

? INVESTIGATE!

Why is it important to have laws of motion that everyone in the world agrees on?

Isaac Newton spent his entire life studying physics. He experimented with forces and motion and developed three ideas, called laws, that explain how forces and motion work. Today, those laws are known as Newton's laws of motion. They explain how forces and motion work together on everything in the universe.

NEWTON'S FIRST LAW OF MOTION

Newton's first law of motion states, "An object at rest will remain at rest unless an **unbalanced force** acts upon it. In the same way, an object in motion will stay in motion unless an unbalanced force acts upon it."

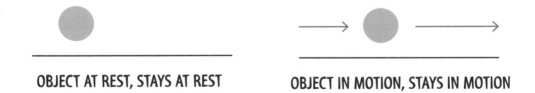

OBJECT AT REST, STAYS AT REST

OBJECT IN MOTION, STAYS IN MOTION

Newton's first law means that forces are needed to change the way things move. For example, a soccer ball that is just sitting on the field will not move on its own. The ball will stay on the field in the same place for a very long time. If you kick it, the ball will sail into the air and possibly into the goal.

Your foot provides the unbalanced force that makes the soccer ball move. An unbalanced force is a force that does not have a **mirroring force**. A mirroring force is one that sends the object back.

inertia: the resistance of any object to a change in state or motion.

WORDS TO KNOW

The tendency of an object to resist a change in movement is called inertia. Newton's first law of motion is sometimes called the law of inertia. The law of inertia applies to pretty much every object we can think of—trains, boats, cars, even rockets. All of those devices cannot move unless they have a force that gives them a push.

In most cases, it is some kind of energy, or power, that makes the vehicles go. For example, a car moves when you push on the gas pedal because this gives the engine fuel for energy. The energy provided by the engine creates the force that moves the car forward. This is true for trains and boats, too.

WHAT DO PHYSICISTS LIKE MOST ABOUT BASEBALL GAMES?

HA HA HA HA

The wave.

HOLD UP THAT WALL!

An example of a balanced force would be the force you make when you push against a wall. Give it a try. Stand up. Put both hands against the wall. Now push hard. Does the wall move? No. The force that you apply to the wall is balanced by the force that the wall pushes back on you. That's why the wall doesn't move.

Let's try an unbalanced force. Push a book across the table. Does the book move? Since your push is greater than the frictional force from the table opposing your push, the total force applied is unbalanced and the book moves.

stationary: not moving.

WORDS TO KNOW

Newton's first law doesn't just apply to things that are **stationary**, or standing still. It can also be used to describe objects that are already in motion.

Once an object is set into motion, it tends to stay in motion. For example, a bike rolling down the street will keep rolling down the street until you stop it with brakes. A moving bike has inertia, which means that it will keep moving at the same speed unless a force is applied to it.

However, if you never used the brake when coasting on your bike, you still wouldn't coast forever. The wheels on the bike experience friction as they travel across the road. That friction is an unbalanced force and will eventually slow the bike down.

Did You Know?

Inertia is the reason seatbelts are important. When the driver slams on the brakes, the car slows down, but you don't. Your seatbelt provides the force to make you stop moving.

If you kick a ball on the grass, will the ball roll forever? Why not?

FRICTION IN SPACE

Inertia is very important in space. Objects in space travel according to the laws of physics, just as they do here on the earth. However, there is less friction in space. There isn't air resistance to slow things down, as there is on the earth. Objects in space tend to keep moving in a straight path unless they encounter a force. If your spaceship wants to go on a straight path, that's a good thing. What if you want to turn around or change direction? You need a force—a blast from the ship's engine—to change the direction of the spaceship.

PS Watch astronauts at the International Space Station prove Newton's laws of motion!

KEYWORD PROMPTS

Newton's laws space station

When an object is moving, it is said to have momentum. Momentum is mass in motion. The heavier the object, or the greater the mass, the greater its momentum. Inertia is also affected by the mass of the object. Something that has a huge momentum will also have a huge inertia. The more inertia an object has, the greater the force needed to stop it. A moving subway train that weighs more than 452,000 pounds will take an enormous amount of energy to stop!

WORDS TO KNOW

momentum: the tendency of a moving object to keep moving.

velocity: the rate at
which an object changes
its position.

NEWTON'S SECOND LAW OF MOTION

Newton's second law of motion states,
"Acceleration is produced when a
force acts on a mass. The greater the mass (of the object
being accelerated), the greater the amount of force needed (to
accelerate the object)."

OBJECTS WITH MORE MASS REQUIRE MORE FORCE TO MOVE

Acceleration is the change in speed, or **velocity**, of an object
over time. Speed is the rate of motion, or how fast something
is traveling. For example, the speed a car travels might be 30
miles per hour.

Velocity is speed plus direction. That means when you talk
about velocity, you use the speed the object is traveling and
also the direction. For example, you might say, "The car is going
north at 30 miles per hour."

Acceleration is the rate of change of velocity. If something
is accelerating, either its speed is changing or its direction is
changing. For example, the car's speed might accelerate from 30
miles per hour to 45 miles per hour. Another way for the car
to accelerate is to turn east instead of continuing north. Both
a change in speed and a change in direction show acceleration.

Imagine that a race car is driving around a rectangular track. As the car starts out, it is driving at 50 miles per hour. The driver presses on the gas pedal and the car slowly increases its speed to 75 miles per hour. The car is accelerating because it is going faster and the increase in speed took a few seconds to happen.

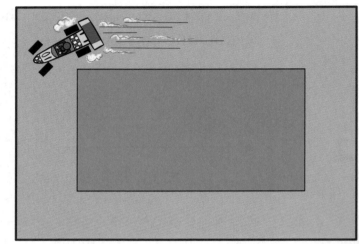

Let's say the car maintains that same 75 miles per hour speed as it goes around the track. Is it still accelerating? What if it slows down each time it goes around a corner?

Newton's first law states that the greater the mass of an object, the more inertia it has. That makes heavy objects such as a subway train hard to stop. Newton's second law also says that the more mass an object has, the more force is required to move it. It takes more force to lift or push or pull a heavier object.

Think of a box full of library books. Can you pick it up by yourself? Maybe. But you probably have to bend your knees and use a lot of effort to lift it. What if the same box was empty? Would it be easier to lift?

Newton's second law is described by the following equation: **force equals mass times acceleration, or f = ma.**

✳ f is the force required to make the object move

✳ a is the acceleration of the object.

✳ m is the mass of the object

CRUISING DOWNHILL

Acceleration does not always require a push or a pull, but there has to be some kind of **external force**. Imagine riding a bicycle down a hill. As you go down the hill, the bicycle speeds up, or accelerates. Why? You aren't pedaling any faster. Gravity is acting on the bicycle and, of course, on you. Gravity is the force that is causing the bicycle to increase acceleration as it goes down the hill. Unless you apply the brakes, you will keep going for quite a while. The inertia of the bicycle will keep the wheels turning. Enjoy the ride!

Watch physics in action at the circus in this video.

WORDS TO KNOW

KEYWORD PROMPTS

circus physics Newton's laws 🔍

NEWTON'S THIRD LAW OF MOTION

Newton's third law states, "For every action there is an equal and opposite re-action." This means that for every force, there is an equal force in the opposite direction.

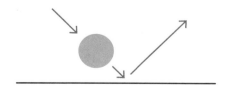

AN OBJECT REACTS TO FORCE WITH AN EQUAL AND OPPOSITE REACTION

WORDS TO KNOW

When you push someone on a swing, you are applying a force to the person. What happens? They swing forward. Then they swing back. Why do they swing back? The motion of the swing coming back at you is the opposite force, or reaction, of your push. If you push the person harder, the force coming back at you will be equally as hard. Watch out!

Newton's third law is the reason rockets work. Imagine a rocket standing on the launch pad. A rocket is a big cylinder with a huge engine at the bottom. As the countdown begins, the fuel in the engine **ignites.** You see big flames and lots of gas and smoke come out from the bottom of the rocket. The countdown continues until 3 . . . 2 . . . 1 . . . blastoff!

The rocket slowly begins to rise. As it goes up, the fire and smoke stream out of the bottom nozzles on the rocket, creating **thrust.** Thrust is what causes the rocket to rise into the air. This happens because of Newton's third law. For every action, there is an equal and opposite reaction. The gas and air pushed down out of the rocket causes the rocket to rise into the air.

? INVESTIGATE!

It's time to consider and discuss: Why is it important to have laws of motion that everyone in the world agrees on?

NEWTON'S RECAP

Imagine you are on a soccer field. The ball is lying there by your feet. It's not moving. In order for the ball to move, it needs a force to overcome its inertia, or tendency to remain in one place. You kick it. The ball shoots down the field. It bounces off the crossbars of the goal and flies back toward you. You duck, just in time! You pick up the ball and place it in front of your foot. This time you kick the ball really hard. It sails completely over the goal, hits the ground, and keeps on rolling. Eventually, it stops. You just experienced all three of Newton's laws of motion.

Newton's First Law of Motion:
"An object at rest will remain at rest unless an unbalanced force acts upon it. An object in motion will stay in motion unless an unbalanced force acts upon it."

Newton's Second Law of Motion:
"Acceleration is produced when a force acts on a mass. The greater the mass, the greater the amount of force needed."

Newton's Third Law of Motion:
"For every action there is an equal and opposite re-action."

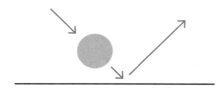

BODY IN MOTION

Newton's second law talks about bodies in motion. Let's see if you can predict where something will fall while it is moving.

1 Place the target on the ground. Walk about 15 feet back from the target and make a mark on the ground.

2 Hold the tennis ball in your hand. Place your elbow next to your side with your hand parallel to the ground.

3 Run at a quick pace from the starting point and try to drop the ball directly onto the target as you keep running past the target.

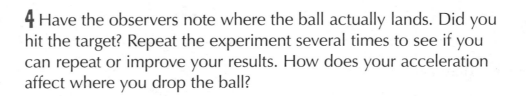

4 Have the observers note where the ball actually lands. Did you hit the target? Repeat the experiment several times to see if you can repeat or improve your results. How does your acceleration affect where you drop the ball?

WHAT IS HAPPENING? How hard was it to guess when to drop the ball so it hit the target? How do you think this would change if the person ran faster? Slower? Give it a try.

SUPPLIES

* small plastic cup
* playing card
* coin

CATCH THAT PENNY!

According to Newton's first law, objects tend to stay right where they are. It takes forces to move them. Watch what happens when you try to move a penny.

1 Put a playing card on top of the plastic cup. Place a coin on top of the card.

2 With a sharp flick of your fingers, push the card out from under the coin, or pull it really quickly toward you. Where does the coin go?

3 Now try it again, this time pulling the card slowly. What does the coin do?

WHAT IS HAPPENING? How did the coin move when you flicked the card quickly versus pulling it slowly? How does Newton's first law apply here? Which forces are at work? What do you think would happen if you balanced the card on your finger with the coin on top? Could you get the penny to balance on your finger? Give it a try!

SUPPLIES

* pair of roller skates or roller blades
* protective gear
* basketball

IT'S NOT ROCKET SCIENCE. WELL, MAYBE IT IS . . .

You don't need a rocket to test Newton's third law of motion. You can do it yourself at home.

1 Put on the skates and protective gear.

2 Hold the basketball in your hands in front of you.

3 With both hands, push the basketball in front of you, or throw it, as hard as you can.

WHAT IS HAPPENING? Did you roll backwards? How did your own body balance the force of you throwing the basketball forward? How is this force like a rocket taking off? Try it with smaller balls to see how that affects your force. How do you think your throw would affect you if were standing on the ground? Would you still move backwards?

Did You Know?

Every time a cannonball is fired, the cannon jumps back, or recoils. This is an example of Newton's third law. The force of the cannonball going forward is offset by the cannon moving backward.

BALLOON BOAT

Buoyancy isn't the only force that acts on a boat. Try this experiment to see how Newton's third law can make the boat go!

SUPPLIES

* 3-inch plastic tube or straw
* small, flat piece of Styrofoam or an empty milk carton
* cork or rubber stopper with a hole
* small and large balloons
* paper clip
* bathtub or wading pool filled with water
* science journal and pencil

1 Insert the plastic tube into the Styrofoam, balsa wood, or milk carton so that the end pokes out underneath. This is your boat.

2 Insert the top end of the tube into the stopper or cork. The stopper needs to have a hole in it.

3 Blow up the small balloon, but don't tie it off. Secure it about an inch from the end with the paper clip to keep the air inside.

4 Place the end of the balloon around the stopper. Then put your boat into the water. On the count of three, pull the paper clip off your balloon. What does the boat do? Write your observations in your science journal.

WHAT IS HAPPENING? According to Newton's third law of motion, for every action, there is an equal and opposite reaction. How is your boat similar to a rocket as it takes off? How would the boat be affected if you used a bigger balloon?

CHAPTER FOUR

MIGHTY MAGNETISM

Magnetism is a force that you deal with every day.
Magnetism keeps your drawers closed, allows you to
hang notes on the refrigerator, and even helps to make
your car and cell phone work. Magnets act by attracting
or repelling certain metals, such as iron and steel.

People have known about magnets for thousands of years. The
ancient Greeks discovered some of the first magnets. These
were called lodestone. The Greeks believed that lodestone was
iron ore that had been struck
by lightning.

? INVESTIGATE!

What are magnets
used for in our world?

Today, we know that lodestone is a form of magnetite. This is a common **mineral**.

The Greeks discovered that if they rubbed a steel needle against lodestone, the needle would then attract other metals. In 1000 CE, the Chinese realized that when a magnetized needle was suspended from a string, it would point along the north–south line. This is how the first compass was created!

> **mineral:** a naturally occurring solid found in rocks and in the ground. Rocks are made of minerals. Gold and diamonds are precious minerals.

PARTS OF A MAGNET

When you put two magnets close together, they either attract or repel each other. The resistance you feel when the two magnets are pushing each other apart is due to the magnetic field. The magnetic field is the invisible area around the magnet. Every magnet has one.

Some magnets have magnetic fields that stretch far out and are very strong. The strength of the magnetic field depends on the strength of the magnet. The stronger the magnet, the stronger the magnetic field.

Every magnet has two poles, one at each end. One is called the north pole and the other is called the south pole. If you push two south poles close together, they repel each other. Two north poles repel each other, too. A north pole and a south pole attract each other. Have you ever heard the phrase, "Opposites attract"? That's certainly true for magnets!

The poles are where the magnets are the strongest. While you can use the middle part of the magnet to attract things, objects are much more likely to be attracted to the ends of the magnet.

A permanent magnet is a magnet that lasts a very long time. Some materials, such as iron, nickel, and cobalt, can be made into magnets, but they will eventually lose their ability to attract and repel objects. Steel is another material that makes a good magnet.

MAGNETIC PLANET

One of the biggest magnets on the planet is right beneath you. The earth is one giant magnet! At the center of the earth is its core. The inner core is pretty much a solid ball of iron, which is a metal that is magnetic. The outer core surrounds the inner core and is made of liquid iron and nickel. Scientists think that the interaction between the inner core and outer core is what controls the earth's magnetic field.

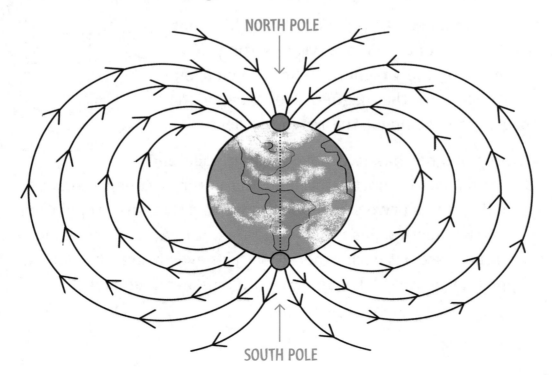

NORTH POLE

SOUTH POLE

As with all magnets, the strongest magnetism is found at the earth's poles. Compasses work because the magnet in the compass needle is attracted to the opposite pole of the earth's magnetic field.

People aren't the only ones who use the earth's magnetic field for direction. Loggerhead turtles, birds, some fish, and even hamsters use the magnetic field to guide them as they move about the earth. Scientists call this ability **magnetoreception**. There is a lot we don't understand about magnetoreception and scientists continue to study it.

MAGNETIC NORTH VS. GEOGRAPHIC NORTH

The earth's magnetic field is created in the core. The magnetic field can shift slightly, depending on the movement of liquids within the core. This can cause the magnetic north of the earth to also shift. The geographic north is always considered to be the northernmost point of the planet. Sometimes, the magnetic north and the geographic north do not line up exactly. This can cause problems if you are using a compass. Usually, the difference is small.

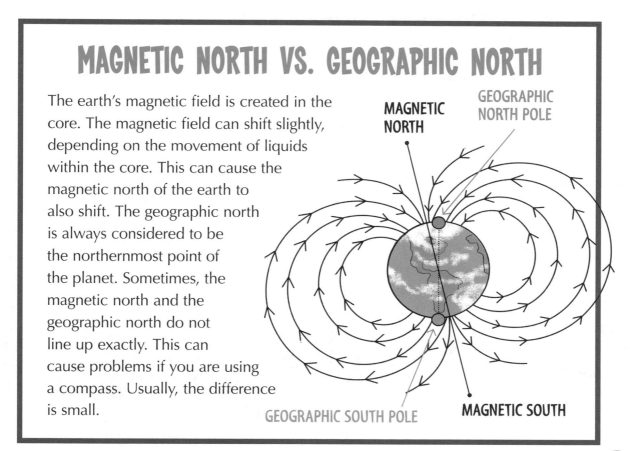

MAGNETIC NORTH

GEOGRAPHIC NORTH POLE

GEOGRAPHIC SOUTH POLE

MAGNETIC SOUTH

solar cycle: the cycle of magnetic activity of the sun.

solar flare: a sudden flash of brightness observed near the surface of the sun.

WORDS TO KNOW

Other planets also exhibit magnetism. Jupiter has one of the largest magnetic fields of any of the planets. Its magnetic force is more than 20,000 times stronger than the earth's.

Saturn, Neptune, and Uranus also have magnetic fields greater than the earth's. But Mars, Mercury, and Venus have weaker magnetic fields.

The sun also has both a north pole and a south pole, just as the earth does. But the sun's poles go through a cycle and actually flip every 11 years!

WHY DIDN'T THE SUN GO TO COLLEGE? It already had a million degrees!

SUNSPOTS

Sunspots are dark spots on the sun. They are caused by very strong magnetic forces on the sun's surface. The sun has a very active magnetic field. During a **solar cycle**, the magnetic activity increases to a maximum peak and then the poles shift. Then the cycle settles down again for another 11 years. During its maximum peak, many sunspots appear. In fact, there can even be occasional **solar flares**, which is when magnetic fields cross over each other, sending plumes of hot liquid plasma high into the air.

  PS **You can see photographs of sunspots here.**

KEYWORD PROMPTS

L – – – – – – – – – → NASA solar cycles 🔍

TYPES OF MAGNETS

Magnets come in all shapes and sizes. Some are strong enough to pick up cars. Others are small and too weak to stick to your refrigerator. The strength of a magnet depends on its shape, size, and material.

Most magnets are shaped like bars and are called bar magnets. The poles are found at each end of the bar, which is where the magnetic field is strongest. Bar magnets are usually made of rectangular pieces of iron or steel. They are permanent magnets, which means they always have a magnetic field. Their magnetism cannot be turned on or off.

Did You Know?

If you cut a bar magnet in half, each new bar will still have a north pole and a south pole.

Bar magnets are not very strong, though, because their poles are far apart. The closer the poles, the stronger the magnet. Bar magnets are used mostly on refrigerators, to close cabinet drawers, and in compasses.

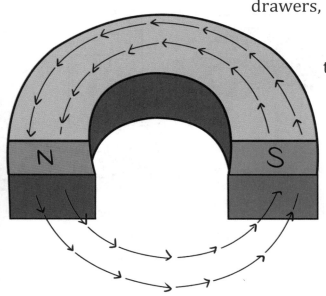

A horseshoe magnet is shaped like the letter U, the same way a metal shoe is shaped to fit a horse's foot. Since its two poles are close together, the magnetic field of a horseshoe magnet is very strong. It is also a permanent magnet. Horseshoe magnets typically have double the lifting strength of a regular bar magnet.

electromagnet: a type of magnet where the magnetic field is produced by electricity.

=**WORDS** TO **KNOW**=

If there are permanent magnets, are there also temporary ones? Yes. You can make some metals into temporary magnets. Simply slide a permanent magnet across the metal several times. The metal will become magnetized. That means that it will act as a magnet for a short time.

ELECTROMAGNETS

When an electric current flows through a wire, a magnetic field is formed. This is called an electromagnet.

Electromagnets can be tiny. If you wrap a bit of wire around a metal nail, you can create an electromagnet. They can also be huge. Have you ever seen the massive electromagnet that is used to pick up cars in a junkyard?

The magnetic field of an electromagnet lasts as long as the electricity is flowing. If the electricity is turned off, the magnetic field disappears. This is handy for when the big magnet in the junkyard needs to drop a car onto a pile.

Many objects contain electromagnets—door bells, trains, cellular phones, and even your computer. Magnetic forces are everywhere.

? **INVESTIGATE!**

It's time to consider and discuss: What are magnets used for in our world?

SUPPLIES

* ✳ tape
* ✳ graph paper
* ✳ several magnets
* ✳ toy car that moves easily
* ✳ science journal and pencil

MAKE THE CAR GO

How far can a magnet's field reach? It might be much farther than you think!

1 Tape the graph paper to a flat surface, such as a table.

2 Tape a magnet to the top of the toy car and set the car on the left side of the graph paper.

3 Hold another magnet behind the car, making sure that it is facing the opposing pole from the magnet on top of the car.

4 Move the magnet closer to the car, very slowly, and count how many squares away it is on the graph paper when the car begins to move. Record this number in your science journal.

5 Stick two magnets together and repeat the experiment. Write down how close the double magnet needs to be in order to move the car.

WHAT IS HAPPENING? The stronger the magnet, the greater the magnetic field around it. Can you see a difference in how close the magnet had to be to get the car to move when using one or two magnets? How far away can you be? Get more magnets and keep trying.

WHAT'S THE ATTRACTION?

Some magnets have magnetic fields that reach really far, but others have smaller magnetic fields. In this activity, you'll do an experiment to find out what type of magnetic field a magnet has.

SUPPLIES

* science journal and pencil
* plastic or wooden ruler
* paper clip
* 2 or more different bar magnets

1 Start a scientific method worksheet in your science journal. Which magnets do you think will have the strongest magnetic fields? You can organize your predictions and results in a chart like the one shown below.

HOW FAR AWAY DO YOU THINK THE PAPER CLIP WILL BE BEFORE IT'S ATTRACTED TO THE MAGNET?

ACTUAL DISTANCE WHEN ATTRACTED (SIZE OF THE MAGNETIC FIELD)

Magnet	Prediction	Result
1		
2		

2 Lay the ruler on a flat, hard surface. Place the paper clip at the end of the ruler so that one side of the paper clip is at the ruler's zero mark.

3 Put one magnet at the other end of the ruler. Holding the ruler in place with your hand, slowly slide the magnet toward the paper clip.

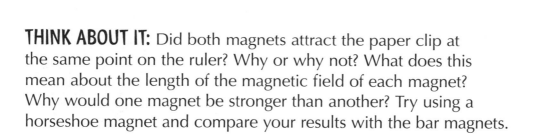

4 When the paper clip attaches itself to the magnet, stop. Note on the ruler where the paper clip and the magnet came together.

5 Record this number in your science journal. Keep track of which magnet you used. Repeat these steps again with the second magnet.

THINK ABOUT IT: Did both magnets attract the paper clip at the same point on the ruler? Why or why not? What does this mean about the length of the magnetic field of each magnet? Why would one magnet be stronger than another? Try using a horseshoe magnet and compare your results with the bar magnets.

PICK UP PAPER CLIPS

Magnetic fields get weaker with distance. With a bar magnet, try to pick up a long chain of paper clips. Which ones are held more strongly, the ones closest to the magnet or farther away? What happens if you rub a paper clip with the magnet? Can it hold other paper clips? Is it a strong or weak magnet? How long does the magnetism last?

CAN YOU SEE THE LINES?

Magnetic field lines are normally invisible, but they are always there. Using tiny metal shavings, you can see the field lines around a magnet. How do you think they will look—straight or curved?

SUPPLIES

* ✱ several paper or plastic plates
* ✱ 3 bar magnets
* ✱ tape
* ✱ 2 tablespoons iron filings, found at your local hardware store or online at a science shop
* ✱ empty salt shaker
* ✱ science journal and pencil

1 Turn one plate over and tape a bar magnet to the center of the bottom of the plate. Turn the plate back over so it's right side up. Put the iron filings inside the salt shaker

2 Slowly shake the iron filings onto the plate in the area directly over the magnet. What kind of pattern do they form? Draw the pattern in your science journal.

3 Repeat steps 1 and 2 with another plate. This time tape two magnets a small distance apart to the bottom of the plate.

4 Before shaking the iron filings, predict what type of pattern you will see. Record your hypothesis in your science journal. Draw the pattern. Are you correct?

atom: a very small piece of matter. Atoms are the tiny building blocks of everything in the universe.

=**WORDS TO KNOW**=

5 Move the magnets around and try the experiment again. What happens if you line up the north poles of each magnet or the south poles of each magnet?

WHAT IS HAPPENING? The iron filings are showing you the pattern of the magnetic field lines for each magnet. Notice how they change as you change the ends of the magnets that are next to each other. Can you tell which end is the north pole just by looking at the filings?

NORTHERN LIGHTS

The Northern Lights in the Alaskan sky are caused when energized particles zoom in from the sun and interact with the earth's magnetic field.

Have you ever looked up at night and seen colored lights shimmer across the sky? These colored lights in the sky are known as the aurora borealis if you live in the Northern Hemisphere, or the aurora australis, if you live in the Southern Hemisphere. The lights are best seen at the far north and the far south of the earth. Charged particles from the sun interact with the **atoms** in the earth's magnetic field. When these charged particles strike the atoms, they excite them, causing the atoms to light up and give off brilliant colors. **You can see pictures of them here.**

KEYWORD PROMPTS

space aurora photos 🔍 ← — — — — ┐

HOVERING HOOPS

Want to make something float in mid-air? Check out this fun experiment to see if you can get the hoops to hover!

SUPPLIES

* 6-inch wooden dowel
* board to hold up your wooden dowel
* glue or tape
* 6 ceramic magnets with holes in the middle (dowel must be able to fit inside the ring of each magnet)

1 Mount the wooden dowel vertically in the center of the base board. If you use glue, you may need to wait a few hours for the glue to dry.

2 Place the first magnet over the dowel and let it fall to the bottom.

3 Take a second magnet and bring it close to the first magnet. Do you feel the forces repelling? If not, turn the magnet over. Which sides of the magnets repel each other?

4 Place the second magnet over the dowel with the like poles facing each other. Does the second magnet lie on top of the first magnet? Or does it appear to float? Repeat steps 3 to 4 until all six magnets are on the dowel.

WHAT IS HAPPENING? Do the magnets appear to float in mid-air? Why do you think this is happening? What would happen if you turned the magnets over?

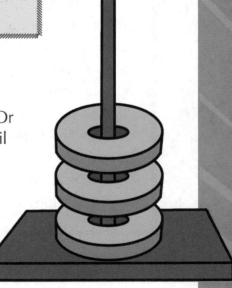

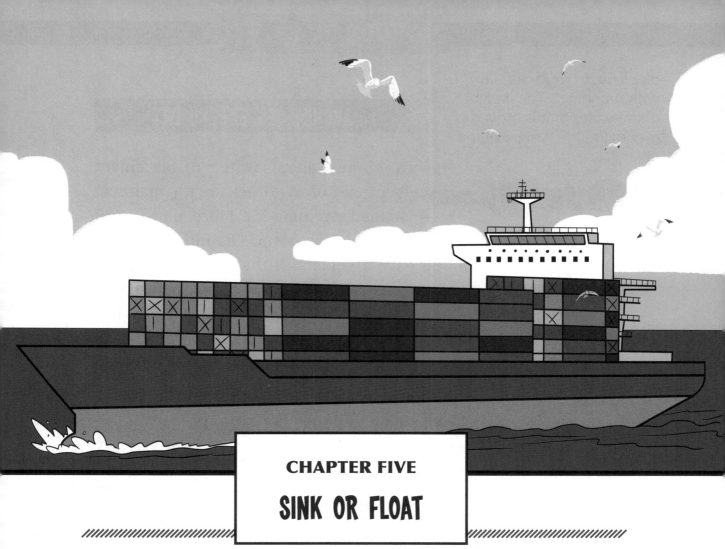

CHAPTER FIVE

SINK OR FLOAT

Have you ever seen a giant ship stacked high with boxes or cars? Massive ships called container ships can carry more than 25,000 tons of cargo. Container ships are also usually made of steel, which is a very heavy material. How does such a heavy ship stay afloat? It's because of buoyancy! This is the force that pushes up on an object as it floats in a liquid. Container ships float because of buoyancy.

cargo: goods carried by ship, truck, train, or airplane.

INVESTIGATE!

What would happen if boats couldn't float?

displace: to replace fluid with an object. The weight of the water that is moved is equal to the weight of the object.

WORDS TO KNOW

ARCHIMEDES' EXPERIMENT

We know about water displacement because of a Greek mathematician named Archimedes. More than 2,300 years ago, Archimedes' king had a problem. The king wanted a new golden crown and gave a goldsmith the gold to make the crown. The king was very excited! But when he was presented with the crown, he knew that something wasn't right. The crown felt too light. The king wondered if perhaps the goldsmith had used some silver in the crown and kept the rest of the gold for himself.

The king asked Archimedes to find out. But how? He couldn't melt the crown down to see what it was made of. Archimedes was stumped. He decided to take a bath and do some more thinking.

EUREKA!

Archimedes filled the tub to the top with water and climbed in. *Whoosh!* Water sloshed over the sides of the tub. He suddenly knew the answer to his problem. The water had been **displaced** by his volume. That meant that the weight of water that sloshed over the side of the tub was equal to the weight of his body as it sank into the tub.

MEET A PHYSICIST!

ARCHIMEDES

Archimedes (287 **BCE**–about 212 BCE) was a Greek mathematician and astronomer. He is best known for developing Archimedes' principle, which explains why some objects float in water and others do not. Archimedes didn't work with just water, though. He also developed geometry. That is a type of math that deals with the size, shape, and volume of objects. He even invented a few **simple machines**. These included a pulley that could lift heavy objects easily and a screw that helped to pump water or liquids. Archimedes was a handy guy to have around!

Archimedes did a test. He took a bar of gold the same size as the one the king had given to the goldsmith to make his crown. Then he placed it in a full tub and measured the amount of water that sloshed over the side. Next, he took the gold crown and repeated the experiment.

Unfortunately for the goldsmith, the amount of water that sloshed over the side of the tub from the crown was not equal to the water from the gold bar. The goldsmith had not used the entire gold bar to create his crown. Instead, he'd used some silver. The king was not happy, but Archimedes was. Learning about displacement helped him develop his principle on buoyancy.

WORDS TO KNOW

BCE: put after a date, BCE stands for Before Common Era and counts down to zero. CE stands for Common Era and counts up from zero. These nonreligious terms correspond to BC and AD. This book was printed in 2016 CE.

simple machine: a tool that uses one movement to complete work.

machine: a device that transmits a force or motion.

density: an object's mass per unit volume.

fluid pressure: the force a fluid exerts by pushing on an object.

volume: how much space an object takes up.

WORDS TO KNOW

WHY DO WE FLOAT?

Humans float in the water for two reasons. First, we have air in our lungs. Air is buoyant. It is lighter than water, which is why a balloon will float in the bathtub and not sink. The other reason is body fat. Fat floats. Muscle and bone do not float. If you have more muscle than you do fat, you might sink. Everyone floats at their own level. Some people float higher, others float at a low level, or not at all. It all depends on their body structure.

DISPLACEMENT AND DENSITY

The principle of buoyancy applies to everything in the water, including beach balls, logs, swimmers, giant ships, and even fish! Buoyancy depends on three things—displacement, **density**, and **fluid pressure**.

As a ship floats in water, it displaces an amount of water equal to its weight. The water that is left under the ship supports it, just as your arms support a puppy when you are holding it. An object's buoyancy is affected by its weight and its density.

An object's density is measured by its mass per unit **volume**. Volume is the amount of space that an object occupies. Density is the relationship between how much something weighs and how much space it takes up.

Imagine a rock that weighs 5 pounds. Will it float? Probably not. It is very dense, meaning that it is quite heavy and solid. The mass of the rock is concentrated in a small space. What if you took a thin sheet of plywood that also weighed 5 pounds?, Would that float?

The rock is much more dense than the sheet of plywood. Density is affected by the surface area, or the total exposed area, of an object. The piece of plywood has much more surface area than the rock. It is less dense and better able to float.

Imagine a ball and ship of the same weight. The bottom of the ship is wider and takes up more space than the ball. This means that the weight of the ship is more spread out. It has a lower density than the ball. Which will float more easily?

Even though the giant ship has all those cars on it, the cars are spread out over the entire ship so that the ship stays afloat. The steel in a ship is flattened out so that it, too, has a low density. The greater surface area and lower density allow the steel ship to float.

Did You Know?

The largest container ship can carry up to 39,000 cars or 117 million pairs of running shoes or more than 900 million cans of dog food. Now that's a lot of stuff!

FLUID PRESSURE

Fluid pressure is the other reason things float. This is the force a fluid exerts by pushing up on an object. Objects float because gravity, the force acting down on them, is equal to fluid pressure, the force pushing up on them. Fluid pressure acts in a perpendicular direction, meaning at a 90-degree angle, to the object.

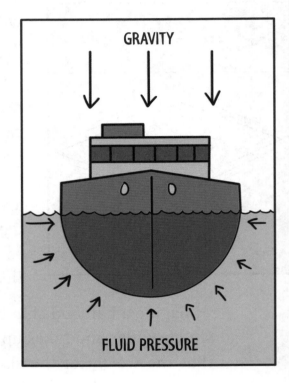

GRAVITY

FLUID PRESSURE

Fluid pressure is dependent upon weight and depth. For example, a heavy ship carrying a huge amount of cars will settle lower into the ocean before it starts to float. If a ship is extremely heavy, it must ride lower in the water in order to meet the point where the two forces balance. The ship will sink to the point where the amount of water displaced is equal to the weight of the ship.

HOW DO LIFE JACKETS WORK?

We use life jackets to help us stay afloat. The foam material inside the life jacket traps air, making the life jackets buoyant. Life jackets don't have to keep you completely out of the water, just your head and shoulders. That is why they are worn like a jacket. If you put them around your legs, your legs would float. But that is not recommended!

KEEP YOUR BALANCE

center of gravity: the average location of the weight of an object.

center of buoyancy: the center of gravity of the water that is displaced by an object.

WORDS TO KNOW

Buoyancy is affected by the overall balance of the object. Think back to the cargo ship. What would happen if all of the cars were loaded on the back of the ship, leaving the front of the ship empty? It would probably start to sink, or perhaps flip over. The two factors that are important in keeping a ship balanced are its **center of gravity** and its **center of buoyancy**. These two things should be perpendicular to each other or in the same place at all times.

The center of gravity of a ship is the single point where all of its weight is acting in a downward motion. Imagine the ship is a seesaw and the cargo is balanced on the ends. If the cargo is placed evenly across the ship, the ship will balance. The center of gravity is the point at which the ship is equally balanced on both sides, just like the center of the seesaw. But if all of the cargo is at one end, that end might sink while the other end of the ship is up in the air.

capsize: to tip over.

submerge: to go under water.

WORDS TO KNOW

The center of buoyancy is the point where the fluid pressure of the water pushes back up on the ship to keep it afloat. While all of the ship feels the force of the water pushing up on it, the center of buoyancy is particularly important. It must be in line with the center of gravity for the ship to float in an upright position. In fact, to remain afloat, the ship's center of gravity must be above its center of buoyancy. If the two centers are not aligned, then the ship could lean to the side or even **capsize** and tip over completely.

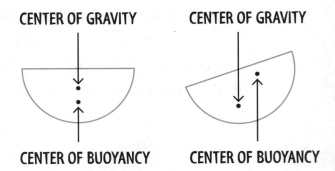

CENTER OF GRAVITY   CENTER OF GRAVITY

CENTER OF BUOYANCY   CENTER OF BUOYANCY

DIVE! DIVE! DIVE!

We want ships to stay afloat, so we make sure the cargo is evenly distributed across the ship. We want a submarine to be able to **submerge**, and also come back up. How can you build a ship that can both sink and rise to the surface?

When a submarine heads out into the sea, it is floating like a normal ship. Its center of gravity is above its center of buoyancy. In order to submerge, the center of gravity must go below the center of buoyancy.

Won't that make the submarine capsize? Not if the two centers are still one on top of the other. The fact that they are in a straight line, one over the other, allows the submarine to stay horizontal and run normally under the surface of the water.

The submarine has a **ballast tank** that makes it possible for the centers of gravity and buoyancy to be rearranged. The ballast tank is a metal tank set inside the outer hull, or the outer shell of the ship. Water can be added to the ballast tank to make the submarine really heavy. As the water rushes in, the density of the submarine increases. What happens to dense objects in water?

ballast tank: a compartment within a boat or submarine that holds water.

WORDS TO KNOW

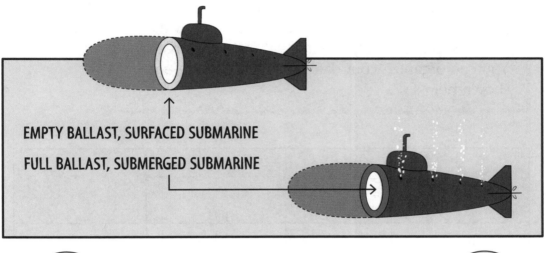

EMPTY BALLAST, SURFACED SUBMARINE

FULL BALLAST, SUBMERGED SUBMARINE

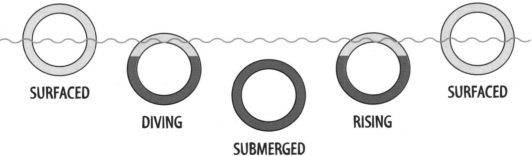

SURFACED

DIVING

SUBMERGED

RISING

SURFACED

When the ballast tanks are about 90 percent full, the submarine is fully submerged. The center of gravity is lower now that the submarine is submerged. This allows the submarine to stay horizontal as it moves through the water.

?

INVESTIGATE!

It's time to consider and discuss: What would happen if boats couldn't float?

67

ARCHIMEDES' GOLD EXPERIMENT

See if you can repeat the famous experiment that Archimedes did to prove that the golden crown was fake. Hint: You don't have to use gold!

SUPPLIES

* science journal and pencil
* graduated cylinder or large measuring cup with measuring lines
* 3 similar sized objects—rocks, pieces of clay, or metal
* scale

1 Start a scientific method worksheet in your science journal. Which of your objects has the most volume? Which one weighs the most? Will the object that weighs the most also be the largest? You can organize your data in a chart like the one shown below.

Object	Mass (weight)	Water Level		Volume (difference in water level)
		before object	after object	
Rock				
Clay				
Metal				

2 Fill the graduated cylinder half full with water. Record the water level in your journal.

3 Weigh each object with the scale and mark its weight down.

4 Drop one of the objects into the water. Check the water level and record this number.

5 Take that object out. Re-check the water level. Make sure you note this in your journal and repeat the process with the other two objects.

6 Calculate the density of each object using this equation:

mass ÷ volume = density

Mass is the weight you measured. Volume is the amount of water displaced. To calculate the volume, subtract the first water level number from the final water level number.

final water level − first water level = volume
20mL − 10mL = 10mL

If your object weighs 25 grams, then your density equation would look like this:

25g ÷ 10ml = 2.5g/mL

WHAT IS HAPPENING? You are calculating the density of each object, just as Archimedes did with the gold. Were the densities different? By how much? Did the objects that weighed more have greater density? What do think would happen if you used a liquid other than water? Try vegetable oil, corn syrup, and salt water. What happens?

IT'S ALL ABOUT THE DENSITY

Play with different shapes to find out what floats best.

SUPPLIES

* modeling clay
* sink full of water
* science journal and pencil

1 Form your modeling clay into a block. Place the block into the sink of water. What happens to it?

2 Mold the block of clay into a ball and place that into the water. What happens? Is there any difference?

3 Try molding the clay into a rounded cup. Test it in the water. Record your findings in your journal.

WHAT IS HAPPENING? As you change the shape of the clay, you are changing the density of your object. Keep trying different shapes. Can you make a shape that floats on top of the water? Can you make a shape that floats below the water, but doesn't sink? How are these shapes and densities different?

TITANIC!

The famous *RMS Titanic* sank more than 100 years ago and yet only recently did scientists learn why. It is believed that an iceberg tore a hole in the back part of the ship. This caused water to flood in and make the stern of the ship very heavy. As the stern grew heavier, it sank under the water and broke away from the front half of the ship.

You can see a computer-generated video of the events researchers believe happened to the *Titanic*.

KEYWORD PROMPTS

National Geographic Titanic sinking 🔍

← — — — — —

MAKE YOUR OWN SUBMARINE

Want to learn how objects can change their buoyancy? Give it a try by making your own submarine.

SUPPLIES

* plastic jug, such as a cleaned-out detergent bottle or soap bottle, with cap
* 8 to 10 heavy coins or weights
* waterproof tape
* flexible straw
* modeling clay
* tub of water

1 Carefully cut three holes in the bottom of the plastic container and one hole in the cap. Get an adult to help you do this.

2 Tape the coins to the bottom of the jug. You should make a stack of four on each side.

3 Put the straw in the cap of the jug and seal around it with modeling clay. The straw should be bent upward like a periscope.

4 Place the jug into a tub of water and watch what happens.

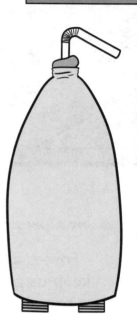

WHAT IS HAPPENING? As the submarine sinks you should see air bubbles rising to the surface. Where are they coming from? Does your submarine float or does it rest on the bottom? How can you get it to float? Can you get it to float at a higher level?

Did You Know?

A submarine can actually go faster under the water than on top of it. The teardrop hull design allows it to cut through water faster, but on the surface, that same hull must work harder to push through the water.

CHAPTER SIX

FORCES AT WORK

Forces are a part of our everyday lives. They help us float, keep us grounded, and point us in the right direction. Forces can also make our lives easier by helping us do work. By using simple machines that work with forces, we can make a small amount of energy do a large amount of work.

? INVESTIGATE!

What simple machines do you use every day to help make work easier?

Machines come in all shapes and sizes. Giant excavators are machines with mechanical arms that dig up huge amounts of dirt. Blenders are machines that mix fruit and yogurt to make smoothies for lunch. Scissors, screwdrivers, and brooms are also machines.

Machines need energy to perform work. They cannot create their own energy. The excavator needs an engine with fuel to provide its energy. The blender uses electricity to power its motor. Even a screwdriver needs a person to provide the energy to make it move.

There are six basic simple machines: the lever, the wheel and axle, the inclined plane, the pulley, the wedge, and the screw.

lever: a bar that rests on a support and lifts or moves things

inclined plane: a flat surface at an angle, such as a ramp.

pulley: a rope on a wheel used to lift things.

wedge: an object that has one thick end and tapers off to a thin edge.

magnitude: how much force is being applied to an object.

MACHINES AND FORCES

Simple machines change small forces into big forces to help do work. Simple machines help us work by doing one of these four things:

* Transferring a force from one place to another
* Changing the direction of the force
* Increasing the **magnitude** of the force
* Increasing the distance or speed of a force

PS **Learn more about using simple machines by playing this video game!**

KEYWORD PROMPTS

Chicago Museum simple machines game 🔍

pivot: the act of turning something.

fulcrum: the point or support where a lever turns.

lever arm: the distance of the lever from the point of the fulcrum.

load: the heavy object that is moved or lifted.

WORDS TO KNOW

LEVERAGING YOUR LEVER

The lever is one of the most basic simple machines. It is a long rigid bar that **pivots** around a single point. Levers use force over a distance to help do work. A lever is made up of three parts: the **fulcrum**, **lever arm**, and **load**.

Have you ever played on a seesaw? A seesaw is made of a lever. The fulcrum is the part that is set into the ground and does not move. The lever arm is the long piece that attaches in the middle to the fulcrum. Kids sit on each end of the level arm when playing on a seesaw. The load is the object the level is lifting. On a seesaw, the load is you and your friends!

Levers have been around for a very long time. Remember Archimedes, who discovered displacement in his bathtub? He was also one of the first people to discover the benefits of using a lever. He figured out that if you used a lever, you could lift heavy things more easily.

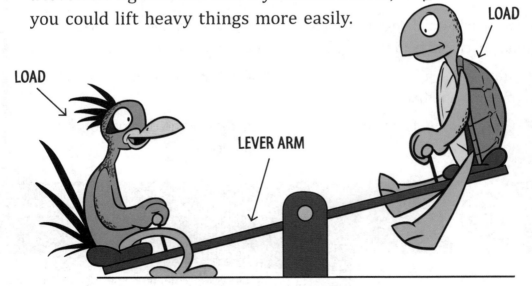

LOAD

LOAD

LEVER ARM

FULCRUM

LETS ROLL!

The wheel and axle have been around since 3500 BCE. The invention of the wheel is said to have completely transformed human life. What would your life be like without wheels? There would be no cars, bicycles, or even wagons for horses to pull.

An axle is simply the bar that fits between the two wheels. This allows the wheels to work together. You find axles on wagons, trucks, and cars. With the wheel and axle, people can carry heavy loads more easily and over a greater distance.

The wheel reduces friction. As you learned earlier, friction is the force that slows things down. If you had to move a heavy box to your friend's house, would you rather slide it down the sidewalk or pull it on a wagon? Which would take less effort?

Did You Know?

Ancient Egyptians used giant wheel-shaped rollers to transport heavy blocks of limestone to make their pyramids. The stone was placed on rollers, scooted forward, and then a roller was brought from behind to the front to keep the stone moving.

UPHILL BATTLE

The inclined plane is another type of simple machine. An inclined plane is a ramp, which is a surface raised on one end at an angle from the ground to a certain height.

You see ramps in lots of different places. They are found at entrances to buildings, in parking garages, and even in roller coasters. Inclined planes help us to move loads more easily to a desired height. The steeper the ramp, the more effort it will take to move the object. Long, low inclined planes work best when trying to move very heavy objects.

WHAT GIVES YOU THE POWER TO WALK THROUGH WALLS?

HA HA HA HA

A door!

More than 5,000 years ago, the ancient Egyptians used ramps to lift blocks of limestone that might weigh 70 tons up the sides of the pyramids.

PULL ME UP!

Pulleys are a type of simple machine that can lift objects straight up. A pulley is made out of a wheel and a rope. One end of the rope fits into the wheel, while the other end is attached to the load, or the object you want to lift. The pulley itself is attached to a structure above the object. When you pull on the loose end of the rope, the pulley helps you lift the object straight toward the wheel.

LENDING A HAND . . . OR A BUCKET

Cranes are designed to lift very heavy loads, such as steel beams for buildings. Cranes actually use a lever-and-pulley system. The long arm of the crane is the lever and the pulley sits at the end of it. The crane uses its engine to reel in the rope and the load rises.

Have you ever lifted a flag up a flagpole? Then you have used a pulley. The pulley itself sits at the top of the pole. You attach the flag to the rope with two clips, then you pull on the other side of the rope. The flag slowly glides up the pole!

tine: a sharp point, such as the ones on a fork.

WORDS TO KNOW

BREAKING THINGS APART

A wedge is a combination of two inclined planes stuck together. Wedges are used to get between two objects and break them apart. The wedge helps focus the energy to a specific point.

Did You Know?

A doorstop is a wedge that is used to hold a door open at a certain position.

Have you ever seen someone using an axe to chop firewood? The axe head has two sides. Both sides start at a wide base and then angle down toward a really sharp edge. If you split the axe head in two, each side would be one inclined plane. To use the axe, the person swings and hits the top of the wood with the axe head. The force of the blow pushes the axe head into the wood, wedging it apart. Now there are two pieces of wood instead of one.

You actually use a wedge every day and probably don't even think about it—a fork! The **tines** on your fork are wedges.

threads: ridges that turn to fasten onto something, such as on a screw.

WORDS TO KNOW

TWIST AND TURN

The last simple machine is the screw. Screws are used to force something into an object by turning. The **threads** of the screw, which are actually inclined planes, are pushed through the object by a twisting force. The power of a screw is how close its threads are. The closer the threads, the more tightly the screw will hold onto the material that surrounds it.

The best example of this is an actual screw. You use a screwdriver to push a screw into a piece of wood. The screw itself grabs onto the wood with the threads. The force you use as you twist the screwdriver forces the screw into the wood. It's the same action you would use when screwing a light bulb into a socket or twisting a lid on a jar.

From gravity to magnetism, buoyancy to simple machines, forces and motion make the world go around. They are involved with everything, from keeping you on the ground to brushing your teeth. You can't live without them!

Did You Know?

Airplane propellers, helicopter blades, and fans are screws that move through the air.

? INVESTIGATE!

It's time to consider and discuss: What simple machines do you use every day to help make work easier?

SIMPLE MACHINES RECAP

Simple machines by themselves have few or no moving parts. They help us to pull, push, lift, and divide. Your muscle power—not electricity or gasoline—makes them work. Simple machines can't do all the work, but they make things easier! This is called a mechanical advantage.

Simple Machine	Common Examples
Lever: a bar that rests on a support and lifts or moves things	Shovel, balance scale, seesaw
Wheel and axle: a wheel with a rod that turn together to lift and move loads. The axle is the rod around which the wheel rotates	Wheelbarrow, bicycle, skateboard
Inclined plane: a flat surface that connects a lower level to a higher level	Ramp, threads of a screw, stairs, hill, ladder
Pulley: a grooved wheel with rope used to lift something or change its direction	Clothesline, flagpole, crane, fishing pole, steam shovel
Wedge: an object with slanted sides ending in a sharp edge that lifts or splits another object	Axe, knife, doorstop, chisel, shark tooth
Screw: an inclined plane or lever wrapped around a pole that pulls one thing toward another	Jar lid, screw, corkscrew, screwdriver, door lock

SUPPLIES

* marker
* Popsicle stick or other type of small, flat piece of wood
* pebbles or dried beans
* quarter

PEBBLES AWAY!

Levers can change the amount and direction of a force depending on the position of their fulcrums.

1 Put the marker on a flat surface. Lean the Popsicle stick on it so that one end of the Popsicle stick is in the air and the other is touching the ground. Which item is acting as the fulcrum?

2 Place one pebble or dried bean on the lower end of the Popsicle stick.

3 Drop the coin on the high side of the Popsicle stick. What happens to the pebble?

4 Move the marker so that it's in the middle of the Popsicle stick. Repeat step 3. What happens to the pebble?

WHAT IS HAPPENING? The position of the fulcrum makes the height of the pebble change. How is this useful for when you need to lift something heavy? Where should you put the fulcrum? Try this out with more pebbles. Is there a change in how far they go?

ROLL LIKE AN EGYPTIAN

Here's your chance to see how the Egyptians used simple machines to help transport heavy blocks of stone to build the pyramids.

SUPPLIES

* newspaper
* heavy book
* piece of string
* duct tape
* flat surface, such as a table or bench
* science journal and pencil
* about 20 to 30 pencils, all the same kind

1 Wrap the book in newspaper. Tape the piece of string to the top of the book.

2 Try to pull the book across the table. Notice how much effort it takes. Record your observations in your science journal.

3 Now line up at least 10 pencils next to each other and place the book on top of them. Pull the book with the string. How much effort does it take? Is it easier than pulling the book without the pencils?

4 Create two teams and see who can pull the books across the table the fastest. What do you learn about the moving pencils?

WHAT IS HAPPENING? Wheels made the job of transporting heavy stones easier for the Egyptians. But they had to find ways to keep the blocks from rolling too far or too fast. How can you keep your book from rolling too fast?

RAMP IT UP!

Ramps make it easier to lift heavy objects. Let's see what you can lift with your ramp.

1 Prop the board at an angle against the books. Tie a string around the object and then tie the string to the rubber band. Place the object at the base of the book stack.

2 Pulling on the rubber band, lift the object straight up to the top of the books. Measure how long the rubber band had to stretch with the ruler. Record the measurement.

3 Now lay the object at the bottom of the ramp. This time pull the object up the ramp and measure how far the rubber band stretched to reach the top. Record your observation.

4 Compare your results. Which method made the rubber band stretch the most? Which way was easier to bring up the object? How do you know?

WHAT IS HAPPENING? Inclined planes help people to do work more easily. Test other objects in your house. Which objects do you find an inclined plane most helpful for when lifting?

WIRE TRANSFER

Do you ever wish you could send something to your friend across the room without getting up and walking? Give this system a try!

SUPPLIES

* 2 empty spools of thread
* 2 pencils
* 40 feet of string
* 2 binder clips or 2 paper clips
* cargo to send your friend, such as a bag of chips or something you can put into a small baggie

1 Place each pencil inside a spool. Give one spool to your friend.

2 Tie the ends of the string together to make a big loop. Loop the string over both spools and have your friend walk as far away as possible, carrying the spool. The string should now be stretched tightly between you.

3 Each of you hold the pencil, not the spool. The spool should be able to spin easily around the pencil.

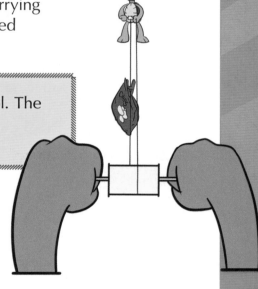

4 Take the bag of goodies and hang it from the bottom string with either the binder clips or the paper clips. Now grab the top string and pull. Keep pulling until the bag reaches your friend.

WHAT IS HAPPENING? You have created a pulley to help you do work. See what else you can send back and forth. Is there a weight limit to what you can carry? How could you make your pulley stronger? Faster?

MADLIB

Use the parts of speech and as many glossary words as you can to fill in the blanks and complete this silly story!

- noun: a person, place, or thing.

- plural noun: more than one person, place, or thing.

- adjective: a word that describes a noun.

- verb: an action word.

- adverb: a word that describes a verb. Many adverbs end in -ly.

Free Falling

Today, I am a scientist and I am observing gravity. When I shake a tree,

a _____ falls to the ground. When I shake the tree _____, lots
   NOUN   ADVERB

of _____ fall to the ground. Why does that happen? Gravity, of course!
   PLURAL NOUN

Sir Isaac Newton discovered gravity when a _____ apple _____ on his
                                            COLOR   VERB

head. He said, "_____!" This is how things work on the earth.
              EXCLAMATION

Can you try it? What else falls due to gravity? _____ or _____
                                               PLURAL NOUN   PLURAL NOUN

or even _____ in space. They all fall due to gravity. Remember that when
          PLURAL NOUN

you are _____ a ball. You don't want to _____ a _____!
         VERB   VERB   NOUN

GLOSSARY

A

accelerate: to change the speed of an object over time.

air resistance: the force of air pushing against an object.

applied force: a force that is applied to an object by a person or another object.

atmosphere: the blanket of air surrounding the earth.

atom: a very small piece of matter. Atoms are the tiny building blocks of everything in the universe.

attract: a force that draws things closer, usually applied to a magnet.

B

ballast tank: a compartment within a boat or submarine that holds water.

BCE: put after a date, BCE stands for Before Common Era and counts down to zero. CE stands for Common Era and counts up from zero. These nonreligious terms correspond to BC and AD. This book was printed in 2016 CE.

buoyancy: the force that makes something able to float in a liquid or gas.

C

capsize: to tip over.

cargo: goods carried by ship, truck, train, or airplane.

center of buoyancy: the center of gravity of the water that is displaced by an object.

center of gravity: the average location of the weight of an object.

centripetal force: the tendency of an object following a curved path to move away from the center of the curve.

compress: pressed or pushed into less space than normal.

contact force: a force that occurs when two objects are touching each other.

D

density: an object's mass per unit volume.

displace: to replace fluid with an object. The weight of the water that is moved is equal to the weight of the object.

E

electromagnet: a type of magnet where the magnetic field is produced by electricity.

energy: the ability to do work.

engineer: someone who uses science, math, and creativity to design products or processes to meet human needs or solve problems.

external force: a force that acts on an object from the outside, such as gravity or the normal force.

F

fluid pressure: the force a fluid exerts by pushing on an object.

force: a push or pull applied to an object.

free fall: the motion of an object being acted upon only by the force of gravity, such as if it were falling from the sky.

friction: a force that slows down objects when they rub against each other. Friction acts in opposition to movement.

fulcrum: the point or support where a lever turns.

G

gravitational force: the force of gravity, measured in Newtons.

gravity: a force that pushes down on objects and also pulls things together in space.

I

ignite: to catch fire or start up an engine.

inclined plane: a flat surface at an angle, such as a ramp.

inertia: the resistance of any object to a change in state or motion.

L

lever: a bar that rests on a support and lifts or moves things.

lever arm: the distance of the lever from the point of the fulcrum.

load: the heavy object that is moved or lifted.

lodestone: a naturally magnetized piece of rock.

GLOSSARY

M

machine: a device that transmits a force or motion.

magnetic field: the space near a magnet where the magnetic force is felt.

magnetism: the force that attracts or repels between magnets.

magnetoreception: a sense that allows an animal to detect a magnetic field.

magnitude: how much force is being applied to an object.

mass: how much matter is in an object.

matter: what an object is made of.

mineral: a naturally occurring solid found in rocks and in the ground. Rocks are made of minerals. Gold and diamonds are precious minerals.

mirroring force: a force that is reflecting back another force.

momentum: the tendency of a moving object to keep moving.

motion: the action or process of moving or changing place or position.

N

normal force: the support force pushing upward on an object from the ground.

O

orbit: the path of an object circling another object in space.

P

perpendicular: when an object forms a right angle with another object.

physics: the science of how matter and energy work together.

pivot: the act of turning something.

pressure: a force acting on a surface from an object or fluid. Air is considered a fluid.

property: a quality or feature of something. The way something is.

pulley: a rope on a wheel used to lift things.

R

repel: a force that pushes things away, usually applied to a magnet.

resisting force: a force that pushes back on an object, usually by air or water.

S

simple machine: a tool that uses one movement to complete work.

solar cycle: the cycle of magnetic activity of the sun.

solar flare: a sudden flash of brightness observed near the surface of the sun.

spring force: a force exerted by a compressed or stretched spring.

stationary: not moving.

submerge: to go under water.

surface area: the total area on the surface of an object.

T

tension force: a force transmitted through a string or rope.

theory: a set of ideas to explain something that has happened.

threads: ridges that turn to fasten onto something, such as on a screw.

thrust: a forward or upward push.

tine: a sharp point, such as the ones on a fork.

U

unbalanced force: a force that has no opposing force. It usually causes movement.

V

velocity: the rate at which an object changes its position.

volume: how much space an object takes up.

W

wedge: an object that has one thick end and tapers off to a thin edge.

weight: the measurement of the pull of gravity on an object.

work: the amount of energy needed to move an object a certain distance.

METRIC CONVERSIONS

Use this chart to find the metric equivalents to the English measurements in this book. If you need to know a half measurement, divide by two. If you need to know twice the measurement, multiply by two. How do you find a quarter measurement? How do you find three times the measurement?

English	Metric
1 inch	2.5 centimeters
1 foot	30.5 centimeters
1 yard	0.9 meter
1 mile	1.6 kilometers
1 pound	0.5 kilogram
1 teaspoon	5 milliliters
1 tablespoon	15 milliliters
1 cup	237 milliliters

WEBSITES

MIKIDS.com Simple Machines: mikids.com/Smachines.htm
Physics4Kids.com: physics4kids.com/files/motion_intro.html
NASA Space Place: spaceplace.nasa.gov/what-is-gravity/en
Explain that Stuff! Magnetism for Kids: explainthatstuff.com/magnetism.html
Ducksters.com Science for Kids: ducksters.com/science

BOOKS

Biskup, Agnieszka. *Super Cool Forces and Motion Activities with Max Axiom*. Capstone Press.

Gore, Bryson. *Physics*. Stargazer, 2009.

Hammond, Richard. *Can You Feel the Force?* DK Pub., 2006.

Hunter, Rebecca. *The Facts about Forces and Motion*. Smart Apple Media, 2004.

Kessler, Colleen. *A Project Guide to Forces and Motion*. Mitchell Lane, 2011.

Silverstein, Alvin, Virginia. Silverstein, and Laura Silverstein Nunn. *Forces and Motion*. Twenty-First Century, 2008.

Spilsbury, Richard, and Louise Spilsbury. *What Are Forces and Motion?: Exploring Science with Hands-on Activities*. Enslow Elementary, 2008.

Uttley, Colin. *Experiments with Force and Motion*. Gareth Stevens Pub., 2010.

QR CODE GLOSSARY

Page 7: youtube.com/user/minutephysics

Page 22: blogs.discovermagazine.com/d-brief/2014/11/06/
watch-feather-bowling-ball-fall-speed/#.VY2hVvlVhBc

Page 29: youtube.com/watch?v=vZYwsAvHgVw

Page 29: youtube.com/watch?v=FQSvowsAUkI

Page 36: youtube.com/watch?v=d1iO-yDp_nA

Page 39: pbs.org/video/1607925512

Page 50: spaceplace.nasa.gov/solar-cycles/en

Page 57: space.com/28857-aurora-photos-northern-lights-2015.html

Page 70: channel.nationalgeographic.com/titanic-100-years/
videos/titanic-sinking-cgi

Page 73: youtube.com/watch?v=2GBky2D7pAA

ESSENTIAL QUESTIONS

Introduction: What is the relationship between force and motion?

Chapter 1: What would it be like to live in a world that had no forces at all?

Chapter 2: Could you live on the earth without gravity?

Chapter 3: Why is it important to have laws of motion
that everyone in the world agrees on?

Chapter 4: What are magnets used for in our world?

Chapter 5: What would happen if boats couldn't float?

Chapter 6: What simple machines do you use
every day to help make work easier?

WHAT GETS WETTER THE MORE IT DRIES?

HA HA HA HA

A towel.

INDEX